PASSPORT TO SOVIET UNION

Stephen Keeler

Franklin Watts

London/New York/Sydney/Toronto

Copyright © 1987 Franklin Watts Limited

First published in Great Britain by
Franklin Watts Limited
12a Golden Square
London W1R 4BA

First published in the USA by
Franklin Watts Inc.
387 Park Avenue South
New York
NY 10016

First published in Australia by
Franklin Watts Australia
14 Mars Road
Lane Cove
NSW 2066

UK ISBN: 0 86313 533 1
US ISBN: 0-531-10495-8
Library of Congress Catalog Card No:
87-50890

Editors: Theodore Rowland-Entwistle
        Jean Cooke
        John Clark
Design: Edward Kinsey
Illustrations: Hayward Art Group
Consultant: Keith Lye

Photographs: Novosti 6B, 6T, 7T, 8T, 9TL, 9TR, 9CL, 9CR, 9LR, 11B, 12T, 13T, 16B, 17TL, 17TR, 18T, 19T, 20T, 22T, 24T, 24B, 25TL, 25B, 28, 29TL, 29TR, 29C, 29B, 30T, 30B, 31T, 31B, 32T, 32B, 33T, 33C, 33B, 34T, 34BL, 34BR, 38T, 38BR, 39B, 40B, 41B, 43B, 44T, 44B, 45TL; Chris Fairclough 20B, 25TR; Hutchison Picture Library 5T, 9B, 13B, 19B, 35T; Stephen Keeler 17B, 21B, 45TR; Kobal Collection 41TR; Popperfoto 42BL, 42R, 45B; John Massey Stewart 7B, 22B, 23B, 42T, 43TL, 43TR; Zefa 5B, 8B, 10T, 10B, 11TL, 11TR, 16T, 18B, 21T, 23T, 35B, 38BL, 39T, 40T, 41TL.

Front cover: Novosti
Back cover: Novosti

Phototypeset by Keyspools Limited
Colour reproduction by Hongkong Graphic Arts
Printed in Belgium

To Vladimir K and Andrei A
with thanks

Contents

Introduction	5
The land	6
The people	8
Where people live	10
Moscow	12
Fact file: land and population	14
Home life	16
Shops and shopping	18
Cooking and eating	20
Pastimes and sports	22
News and broadcasting	24
Fact file: home and leisure	26
Farming and fishing	28
Natural resources and industry	30
Soviet technology	32
Transportation	34
Fact file: economy and trade	36
Education	38
The arts	40
The making of the Soviet Union	42
The Soviet Union in the modern world	44
Fact file: government and world role	46
Index	48

Scale 1:23,000,000
0 200 400 600 800 miles
0 250 500 750 1,000 1,200 km
Chukchi Sea
Bering Sea
East Siberian Sea
New Siberian Islands
Laptev Sea
Severnaya Zemlya
Novaya Zemlya
Kara Sea
Barents Sea
Murmansk
FINLAND
Tallinn
POLAND
Riga
Vilnius
Leningrad
Minsk
Lake Lagoda
Lake Onega
Archangel
Lvov
ROMANIA
Dneiper River
Kiev
Moscow
Odessa
Kharkov
Gorky
Gora Narodnaja
Dnepropetrovsk
Donetsk
Kazan
Black Sea
Don River
Volga River
Perm
Ural Mts
Kuibyshev
Sverdlovsk
Ob River
Ufa
Volgograd
Ural River
Chelyabinsk
TURKEY
Mount Elbrus
Tbilisi
Caspian Sea
Yerevan
Baku
Omsk
Irtysh River
Novosibirsk
Yenisei River
Angara R.
Bratsk
Lena River
Yakutsk
Kolyma River
Kamchatka Peninsula
Sea of Okhotsk
Neryngri
Sakhalin Island
Aral Sea
Amu Darya River
Sry Darya R.
Lake Balkash
Gora Belucha
Irkutsk
Lake Baikal
Yablonovy Range
Ulan Ude
Amur River
Khabarovsk
Ashkabad
Bukhara
Tashkent
Frunze
Samarkand
Alma Ata
IRAN
Dushanbe
7,495m
Communism Peak
AFGHANISTAN
MONGOLIA
CHINA
Vladivostok
Nakhodka
Sea of Japan
NORTH KOREA
JAPAN

Introduction

The Soviet Union is the world's largest country. It covers about a sixth of the Earth's land surface, and is more than twice the size of the United States or China. Its full name – the Union of Soviet Socialist Republics (USSR) – indicates that it is not one nation but a union of many peoples.

Moscow is the capital not only of the Soviet Union but also of the largest of its republics, Russia. Until 1917 Russia was a monarchy with an immensely rich and powerful royal family. The tsar (emperor) ruled over a nation of mostly illiterate and often starving peasants.

In 1917 a group of peasants, soldiers, students and intellectuals overthrew the tsar and established a revolutionary government, a *Soviet*, in the then capital city of Petrograd. Petrograd is now called Leningrad in memory of the first Soviet leader, Vladimir Ilich Lenin.

From its origins as a group of poor, deprived peoples, the Soviet Union has become the world's first Communist nation and a superpower.

Above: These houses on the shores of Lake Baikal are built to withstand the cold. They are typical of those in the more remote Soviet regions.

Below: Old churches, factories, modern offices and apartments can all be seen in this view of Moscow, the Soviet Union's largest city.

The land

The Soviet Union stretches from west to east almost 10,000 km (6,000 miles) across two continents – Europe and Asia – and eleven time zones. Supper time in Minsk, in Europe, is breakfast time in Vladivostok on the Pacific coast. The country is more than 5,100 km (3,200 miles) from north to south.

In the far north is a treeless, frozen plain, the tundra. In summer the top few centimetres of soil thaws, but below that lies the permafrost, ground that never thaws. In parts of Siberia the permafrost is almost 1,500 m (5,000 ft) deep. The tundra eventually gives way to the great forest belt, the taiga. The northern part of the taiga contains mostly conifers. Farther south the forest is a mixture of coniferous and deciduous trees.

In parts of Siberia – the Asian region of Russia – it is colder in winter than at the North Pole. In Yakutia in northeastern Siberia the winter temperature sometimes drops below −70°C (−94°F). Yet in parts of Soviet Central Asia it is hotter in summer than at the Equator.

Above: No trees grow on the tundra, only small shrubs, grasses and lichens. Even in summer the ground just below the topsoil is frozen solid.

Below: A view of the bleak countryside of Sakhalin Island in eastern Siberia. The mountains are surrounded by taiga, forests of coniferous trees.

The Soviet Union is little more than a colossal plain surrounded by mountain ranges. The Ural Mountains in the west separate the European and Asian parts of the country. Further east the Pamir and Altai ranges present a formidable barrier along the south. To the east are the Verkhoyansk, Dzhugdzhur and Stanovoi ranges.

There are more than 500 lakes in the Soviet Union, including the world's largest, the Caspian Sea, and the world's deepest, Lake Baikal in southeastern Siberia. The Caspian Sea is a saltwater lake more than 372,000 sq km (143,600 sq miles) in area. Baikal has an area slightly larger than that of Belgium. It is more than 1,600 m (1 mile) deep and contains 20 per cent of all the fresh water on Earth. The water is of a purity unequalled anywhere else.

More than 300 rivers flow into Lake Baikal but only one, the Angara, flows out of it. Altogether the Soviet Union has more than 100,000 rivers.

Above: A view of the Yenisei River as it flows through Krasnoyarsk in Siberia.

Below: The Barsa-Gelmes Desert is a wasteland in Turkmenistan, east of the Caspian Sea.

The people

The Soviet Union is made up of 15 Union Republics – including Russia – 20 Autonomous (self-governing) Republics, 8 Autonomous Regions and 10 Autonomous Areas. The people of these republics and regions belong to more than 100 ethnic groups. They include Slavic, Turkic, Armenian and Georgian peoples, each with their own cultures, speaking 80 languages and 70 dialects, and using 5 different alphabets.

Most people refer to Soviet citizens as "Russians". But only 52 per cent of the people are Russians, citizens of the Russian Republic. However, Russia is by far the largest of the republics, covering about three-quarters of the country. The Russian city of Moscow is the national capital, and Russian is the Soviet Union's official language. It is written in the Cyrillic alphabet which has letters that are written and pronounced differently to those of the Roman alphabet.

The 42,000,000 people of the Ukraine are the second largest group after the Russians. They are fiercely proud of their capital, Kiev.

Above: An old woman and a child from Sakhalin Island. Their features show that they are descendants of original Mongol inhabitants.

Below: People on holiday stroll along the promenade at Yalta, a popular winter resort on the Crimean Peninsula of the Black Sea in the Ukraine.

Above: Nadyezhda Loktaeva from Tallinn, Estonia, is a pilot.

Below: A construction worker from Buryat Autonomous Republic.

Above: Andrei Bogachev is a traffic policeman in Moscow.

Below: Weaver Valentina Golubeva training workers at Ivanovo.

The third largest group are the 12,500,000 Uzbeks. For a short time in the Middle Ages the Islamic nation of Uzbekistan was the most advanced and powerful in central Asia. Reminders of its former glory under its ruthless ruler, Tamerlane, can still be seen in the beautiful cities of Bukhara and Samarkand. The Uzbeks now have the highest standard of living in central Asia. The Armenian republic, between the Black Sea and the Caspian Sea, is a mountainous region whose people won their independence from Ottoman Turks in 1918.

The Baltic republics of Estonia, Latvia and Lithuania are the most European parts of the Soviet Union. They use the Roman alphabet. Their people have a higher standard of living than even the citizens of Moscow and Leningrad.

Although the government discourages religion, all the major world religions are followed in the Soviet Union, including Christianity, Islam, Judaism and Buddhism.

Above: Children in Turkmenistan enjoying a ripe melon.

Below: A street vendor sells sunflower seeds in Uzbekistan.

Where people live

Above: A modern apartment block at Frunze, the capital of Khirgizia, a typical city development.

Below: Two sailors walk down a narrow street in the old quarter of Tallinn, the capital of Estonia.

The Soviet Union has the third largest population in the world, after China and India. Three-quarters of the people live in the European part of the country. More than twice as many people live in towns and cities as in the countryside. There are over 2,000 major towns and cities in the Soviet Union, and every year ten new towns are completed. About 270 cities have more than 100,000 people, and 22 have 1,000,000 or more.

In the country, increased mechanization and improved efficiency in agriculture mean that fewer farm workers are needed than in the past. Most people, especially the young, want to live in or near a town where living conditions and leisure facilities are usually better.

Migration to the towns has produced serious labour shortages in some of the more remote areas. The government offers better facilities to attract people willing to live in eastern Siberia and develop the area's natural resources.

During World War II nearly 1.2 million Soviet houses and apartment buildings were destroyed. Although 2,000,000 new apartments are built each year, 20 per cent of city dwellers still have to share their homes with another family.

Most Soviet citizens live in cities or towns in apartments or small houses rented from the state authorities. Those who do own their own home may not sell it for more than it cost to buy, but they are allowed to exchange it, rent it out or pass it on to their children. Some families have to wait several years before getting their own apartment.

Moscow is the most popular destination for people wanting to leave the countryside. To avoid overcrowding, the authorities issue only a limited number of residence permits. No one may live in Moscow without such a permit. Only a job in the city or marriage to a Muscovite guarantees the right to residence. Some marriages – sometimes followed by speedy divorces – are arranged merely in order to secure residence permits.

Left: A view over the old part of Baku, the capital of Azerbaijan, towards one of the new quarters.

Above: Houses at Listvyanka, a village near Irkutsk on the shores of Lake Baikal.

Below: A motorized sledge roars over the snow in the Kamchatka Peninsula of eastern Siberia. Such sledges have made life easier in the harsh climate.

Moscow

Moscow has been the capital of the Soviet Union since 1918. Eight hundred years ago settlers on the north bank of the Moskva River, where Moscow stands today, built a *kreml*, a walled fortress. Inside the walls were the most important buildings, such as churches, a palace and arsenals. Several Russian cities began as kremlins (the English form of *kreml*).

The Moscow Kremlin is the seat of the national government. In it are magnificent domed churches and cathedrals, a former royal palace, museums and government offices. The Kremlin Palace of Congresses, built in 1961, is the meeting place for the Supreme Soviet – the Soviet Union's parliament – and for the Communist Party's congresses. It is also used for many other activities, such as concerts, ballets and operas.

Moscow is a city of theatres, concert halls, cinemas, museums and libraries. Two buildings provide a permanent home for the Moscow State Circus. Muscovites think of themselves as the most cultured people in the Soviet Union.

Above: St. Basil's Cathedral, Red Square, in the heart of Moscow, is made up of nine chapels each with its own elaborately decorated roof.

Below: Some of the landmarks of Moscow. They show the contrast between the old part of the city and the new capital.

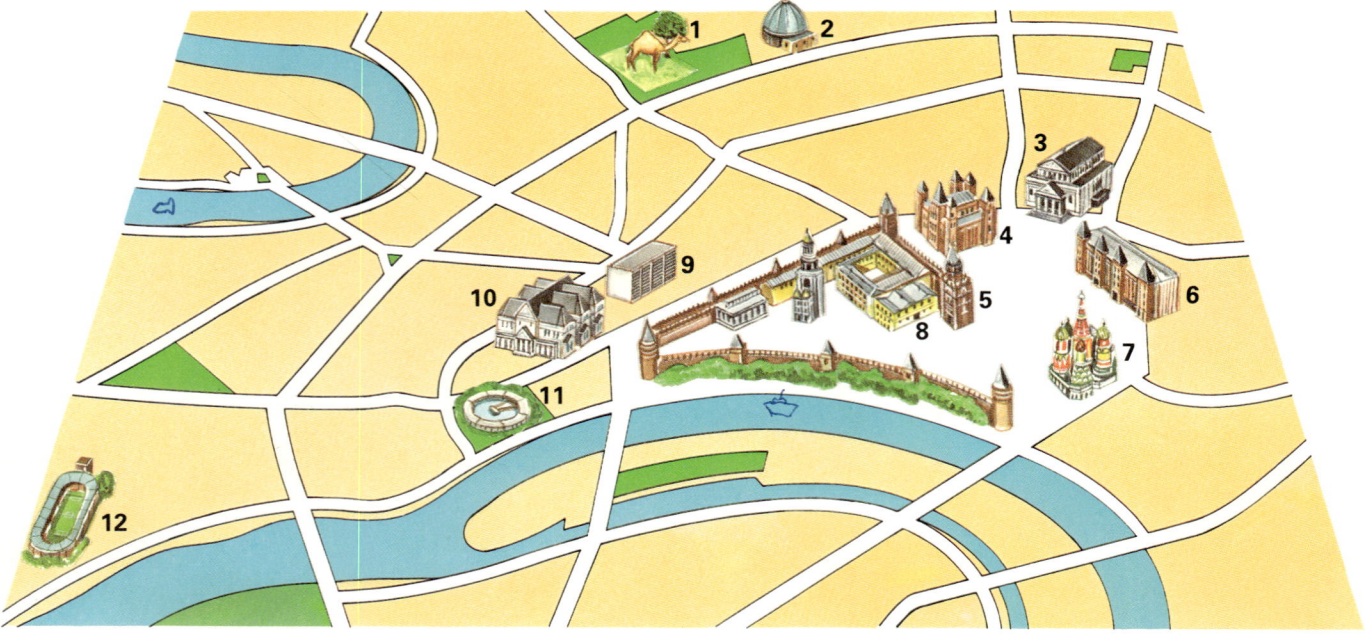

1. Zoo
2. Planetarium
3. Bolshoi Theatre
4. Museum
5. Red Square
6. Gum
7. St. Basil's Cathedral
8. The Kremlin
9. Library
10. Fine Arts Museum
11. Swimming Pool
12. Sports Stadium

Northeast of the Kremlin is Red Square, where a parade is held every November 7 to mark the anniversary of the October Revolution in 1917. Every May 1 workers and children celebrate International Labour Day. In a mausoleum beneath the Kremlin's eastern wall is the embalmed body of Lenin, seen by more than 1,000,000 visitors a year.

The Moscow Metro is the most elegant underground rail line in the world. Its 123 stations, decorated with marble, granite and crystal, are kept spotless by armies of cleaners. It carries about 10,000,000 passengers a day along its 203 km (126 miles) of track.

Muscovites eat 170 tonnes of ice cream every day, even when winter temperatures drop to −10°C (14°). They are also animal lovers who keep thousands of cats, dogs and birds. Like other Soviet city dwellers, they like to spend much of their leisure time in the surrounding countryside. Some are lucky enough to own a *dacha*, a country cottage.

Above: Arbat, in the older part of Moscow, was the first street in the city for pedestrians only. In nice weather it is full of people shopping.

Below: Even in late spring snow, Moscow citizens like to drink their coffee or chocolate at an open-air café.

Fact file: land and population

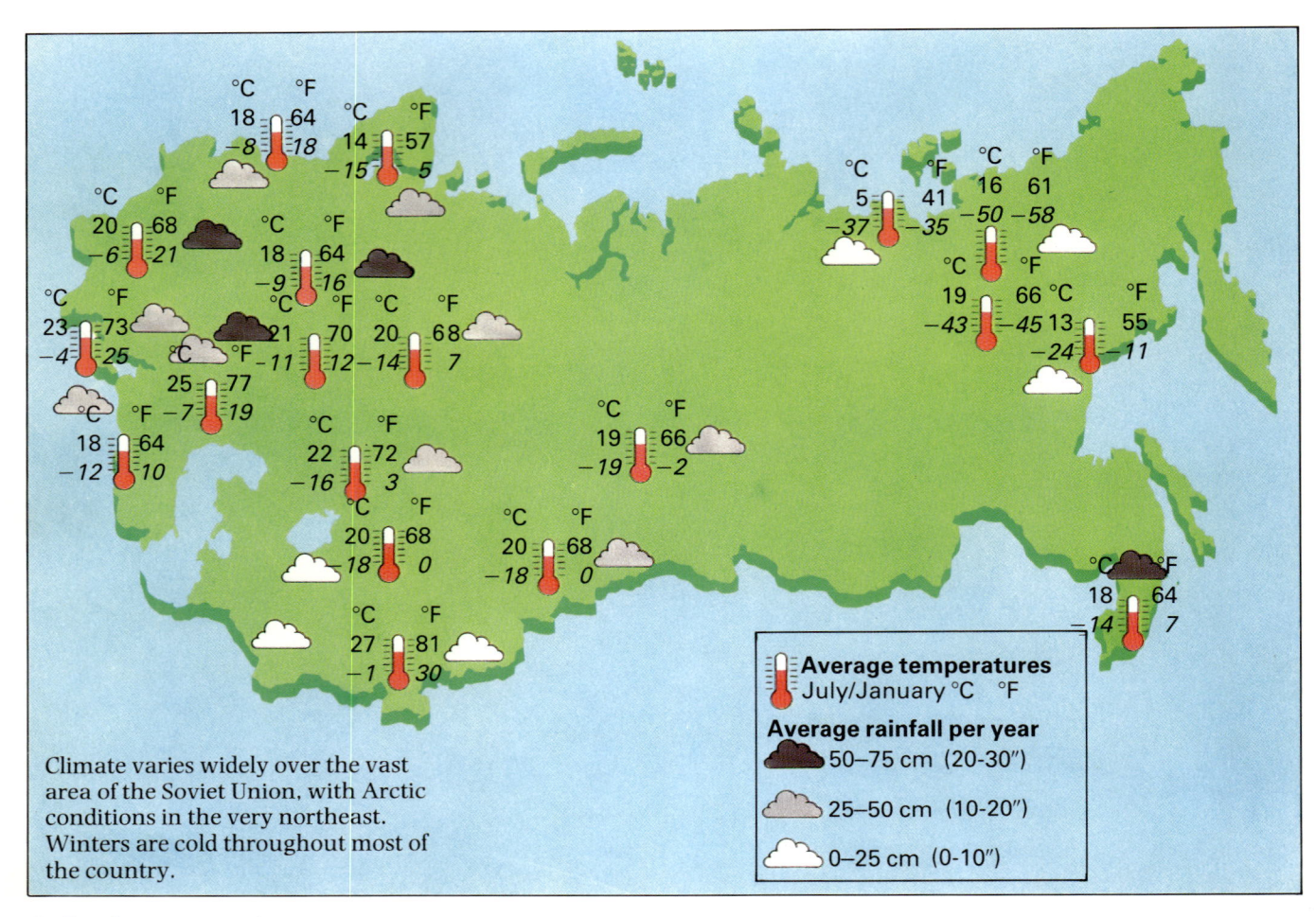

Climate varies widely over the vast area of the Soviet Union, with Arctic conditions in the very northeast. Winters are cold throughout most of the country.

Average temperatures July/January °C °F

Average rainfall per year
- 50–75 cm (20-30")
- 25–50 cm (10-20")
- 0–25 cm (0-10")

▷ **Land area comparison**
With an area of 22,402,200 sq km (8,649,538 sq miles), the Soviet Union is more than twice as big as the United States and 90 times larger than the United Kingdom.

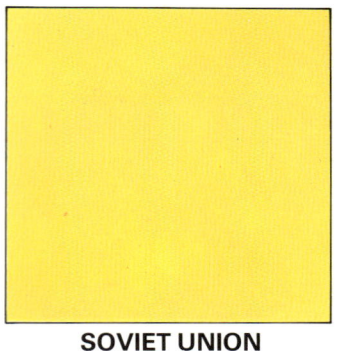

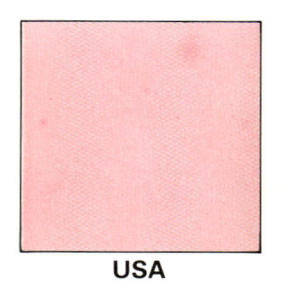

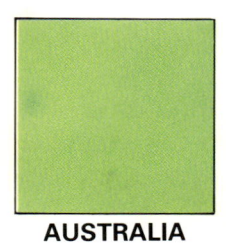

SOVIET UNION　　USA　　AUSTRALIA　　UK

Key facts

Location: The Soviet Union, the world's largest country, straddles Europe and Asia. The mainland extends roughly between latitudes 35° and nearly 78° North, and between longitudes 20° East and 170° West.

Main parts: The country consists of 15 republics. The Russian Soviet Federal Socialist Republic (RSFSR; capital Moscow) is the largest.

Area: 22,402,200 sq km (8,649,538 sq miles).

Population: 279,904,000 (1986).

Capital: Moscow.

Major cities:
Moscow (8,642,000)
Leningrad (4,867,000)
Kiev (2,448,000)
Tashkent (2,030,000)

Highest point: Pik Kommunizma (Communism Peak), 7,495 m (24,590 ft) above sea level in the Pamir Mountains of Tadzhikistan.

Longest river (entirely within the Soviet Union): Lena, 4,400 km (2,734 miles); (in the European part) Volga, 3,531 km (2,194 miles).

Largest lake: Caspian Sea, which covers 370,370 sq km (143,000 sq miles).

Soviet Union 12 per sq km

USA 25 per sq km

Australia 2 per sq km

Britain 231 per sq km

Japan 320 per sq km

France 100 per sq km

▽ **Where people live**
Twice as many people live in towns and cities as in the country.

Urban 66%   **Rural** 34%

◁ **A population density comparison**
The Soviet Union has a very low population density in world terms. Among major nations, only Australia's is lower.

△ **Major population centres**
Most of the Soviet Union's large cities are located in the west of the country, in the major industrial areas.

- Major cities
— Major routeways

Home life

Throughout the Russian and European republics of the Soviet Union the birth rate is so low that married couples without children have to pay a "childless tax" to encourage them to start a family. One reason for the low birth rate is the shortage of good housing in inner cities. Many newly married couples have to live with parents for several years before they can find a home of their own. Most new housing is being built up to an hour's journey by public transportation from city centres.

The average family apartment in the Soviet Union has two rooms, used for both living and sleeping. The apartment also contains a small eat-in kitchen, a bathroom, a toilet, a small entrance hall and perhaps a balcony. Ninety per cent of all Soviet families have a refrigerator. Two-thirds have a washing machine and 22 per cent have a vacuum cleaner. Almost all families have a television set, though most are black and white.

Above: An Uzbek father and his family on the doorstep of their home in Samarkand. The Uzbeks are descended from the westernmost people of the old Mongol Empire.

Right: Weddings are a time for celebration in Moscow, even though the ceremony may be a brief one at a State Wedding Palace.

Skilled workers earn an average of 190 roubles a month. Most workers pay 7 per cent income tax, and members of the Communist Party pay a monthly fee of 6 roubles. In most families both husband and wife have full-time paid jobs outside the home, and for this reason one in four babies under two years old spends up to 12 hours a day in nursery schools, which are free to those on low incomes.

Some 85 per cent of all Soviet women between the ages of 16 and 55 have regular full-time jobs; 70 per cent of all doctors are women, and the Soviet Union has more women engineers than all other countries put together.

Ways of life in the Central Asian and Far Eastern republics have changed little under Soviet influence, although standards of education, health, hygiene and nutrition have risen sharply. Modern Turkmen and Uzbek houses still have a *dastarhan* (raised platform) in one room where families of up to 30 spread their quilts, and nomadic Mongolians of southern Siberia still live in skin tents called *yurts*.

Above left: Birthdays are a time for celebration. Here a grandmother poses for a photograph surrounded by her children and grandchildren.

Above: A five-year-old's birthday party in her family's Moscow apartment.

Below: Cats are popular family pets among people who live in cities.

Shops and shopping

Shopping in the Soviet Union can be an exhausting business. Until recently all shops used the "three-line" system. Under it, customers line up to order the goods they want to buy. The shop assistant removes the goods from the shelf or display case, writes the order on a ticket and hands it to the customer. The customer then waits at the cash desk to pay for the goods. The cashier takes the money and stamps the ticket. The customer returns to the sales counter for another long wait to give the stamped ticket to the assistant, who hands over the goods, usually wrapped in paper and tied with string.

This tedious and time-consuming system is still used in many toyshops, bookshops and some clothes shops and food stores. It has been replaced in the large department stores and new food supermarkets in some of the larger cities by the Western system of paying at the counter or check-out. But a Soviet newspaper once estimated that 30,000 million hours a year are spent by Soviet women just waiting at shops.

Above: Two girls examine baskets of fruit at a street market in Tashkent, the capital of Uzbekistan. Orchards surround this ancient city in the heart of Central Asia.

Left: An open-air market in front of a ruined mosque at Bukhara, in Uzbekistan. Street markets for fresh fruit and vegetables are common in many parts of the Soviet Union.

Left: Inside Cheryomushki supermarket in Moscow. In such supermarkets the Western system of paying at check-out desks has been introduced, which cuts down on shopping time.

Below: GUM is Moscow's largest department store. It stands on Red Square, opposite the Kremlin. GUM stands for Gosudartsvenniy Universalniy Magazin (State Department Store).

There are no real shortages of essential foodstuffs or most basic consumer goods in the Soviet Union, but supplies can be very erratic. For example, bananas may be available one day and then be out of stock for three weeks.

Retired grandmothers are useful for shopping. While the rest of the family is at school or at work these older members can search the shops and markets for newly delivered foodstuffs.

Although such searching is becoming less necessary as food distribution improves, few women – who do most of the shopping – go out without carrying a bag so that they can take advantage of unexpected supplies in the stores.

The average family income is between 400 and 580 roubles a month, depending on the number of working members of the family. Since the 1960s most people's wages have quadrupled, and spending on goods, such as clothes, radios, cameras and cars, has tripled.

Cooking and eating

The food eaten by most Soviet citizens is traditional. It reflects their various ethnic origins – though pizza and hamburger bars are now appearing in Moscow.

Breakfast is a quick, light meal. It may consist of slices of rye bread, a piece of cheese and tea. Dinner, the main meal of the day, includes a meat dish with potatoes and other vegetables. This may be followed by a simple dessert of fresh fruit or cake. Soviet people are fond of meat, so supper will probably include another meat dish, after a bowl of *shchi* (a cabbage soup). People eat large quantities of bread and drink sweet black tea with most meals.

No Russian table is complete without its samovar, an urn in which water is boiled to make tea. The teapot itself usually sits on top of the samovar to keep hot.

Above: A selection of the kind of foods that Soviet people like to eat. They include fresh salads, roast pork and a mug of rich soup.

Right: A typical family meal in the Soviet Union. The samovar which dominates the table is a common sight. People in all the Soviet republics drink sweet black tea.

Left: Food being served at an outdoor communal meeting place at Bukhara, in Uzbekistan. Most of the people speak Tadzhik, which is a form of Farsi (Persian).

Below: A poster warning against alcoholism. Soviet citizens used to drink more hard liquor than people in many other countries.

Traditional Russian dishes include *borscht*, a pungent soup made with chopped beetroot, onions, tomatoes, shredded cabbage and diced sausages. Meat stock, herbs and slivers of mutton or beef are added, and the borscht is served with sour cream. It may be followed by hot *pirozhki* (meat pasties) and sweet *bliny* (pancakes with jam and sour cream).

In Central Asia the people eat soft *naan* bread, baked in clay ovens. Uzbeks, Kazakhs and Turkmen eat a good deal of rice. A typical dish of this region is *palov*. Carrots and onions are fried in vegetable oil; small pieces of mutton are added, and mixed with boiled white rice. Beef and pork are the meats of the north; mutton is more popular in the Asian republics.

Traditionally meals were washed down with iced vodka. Until recently Soviet citizens drank more alcoholic spirits than any other people – an average of 14 litres (25 pints) a year for every person aged over 15. In 1985 the price of vodka was quadrupled as part of the government's intensive anti-drinking campaign. The campaign has been successful in the towns, but less so in the countryside where illegal vodka is distilled.

Pastimes and sports

Chess is the most popular pastime in the Soviet Union, and millions of people learn to play the game to a high standard at an early age. In summer open-air chess games in parks or on quiet street corners are a common sight. They attract large crowds of spectators, young and old, who follow each move with fascination. The country has produced many grandmasters and about a dozen world champions, among them Gary Kasparov and Anatoly Karpov. Karpov is a devotee of another popular Soviet pastime, stamp collecting. There are 5,000 stamp clubs, with a total of more than 400,000 members.

More than half of the world's cinemas are in the Soviet Union, and millions of people flock to them every week. The film industry produces about 180 feature films a year. Most are in Russian, but they are sub-titled or dubbed into ten of the other Soviet languages. The thousand or more museums in the Soviet Union are also popular attractions with families.

Above: In warm weather people flock to lakesides and the Soviet Union's few beaches to swim. Some people even bathe in ice-covered rivers.

Below: Soccer is popular throughout the Soviet Union, from local teams that play in parks to the country's successful international teams.

Left: Lakes in Siberia freeze solid in winter and are safe for children to play on. Here a group of children are skating, sleighing and trying to play ice hockey.

Below: Spectators take a keen interest as people play chess at Gorki Park, Moscow.

More than half the people take an annual holiday away. Moscow and the sunny Black Sea resorts are the favourite places. Travel is relatively cheap. Travel companies belong to the state or such organizations as trade unions.

Organized sports play an important part in the daily life of most Soviet citizens. There are 272,000 physical training clubs, with 93,000,000 members. The country has 80,000 sports halls, 3,800 swimming pools and 3,800 stadiums, all of which are open free to all citizens. It is hardly surprising that the Soviet Union wins so many medals for sport and gymnastics in international competitions. Track and field events, volleyball, skiing, soccer, and basketball are the most popular sports.

The smaller republics have their own traditional forms of exercise, and hold national games every year. The Yakuts of central Siberia are skilled reindeer-sled racers. The mountain farmers of Tadzhikistan race on yaks. Archery is popular with the Buyats of eastern Siberia, and on the Amur River canoeing is popular.

News and broadcasting

Before 1917 more than 75 per cent of the Russian people were illiterate. Today almost everyone can read. People spend, on average, almost one-sixth of their free time doing so. To meet this demand, the Soviet Union is the world's largest producer of newspapers, magazines and books.

The Soviet government believes that the Press has an important part to play in the political and moral education of the people. There are two main daily newpapers. *Pravda* ("Truth") is the official newspaper of the Communist Party. *Izvestia* ("News") is the government paper.

The Soviet news agency TASS provides much of the material for newspapers and magazines. Nothing is published which is thought to be obscene, offensive, or anti-Soviet – though one magazine, *Krokodil*, occasionally criticizes government policy, exposes corruption or campaigns for popular causes. Newspapers and magazines have a more serious content than many in the West.

Above: Vladimir Nazarov, a reporter with the Soviet radio organization Mayak, interviews workers on the 24th floor of a new apartment building under construction.

Below: Presenters Aza Likhitchenko and Igor Kirilov in a Moscow television studio. Soviet television emphasizes serious and educational programmes.

Above left: A selection of children's books, ranging from fairy tales to how-to-do-it books.

Above: Soviet readers have plenty of magazines to choose from, covering all topics from serious political reading to tabloids.

Below: Some of the Soviet Union's daily newspapers. More than 9,000,000 copies of *Izvestia* (top left), are sold daily.

Soviet radio and television are also more serious than those of the West. They broadcast many news and documentary programmes, classical music, sport, and cartoons for children. All violence is censored, and most programmes are broadly educational. People do occasionally complain about the lack of light entertainment.

There are four main television channels. Programmes are broadcast on a relay system. When it's 9 p.m. in Moscow it's already 4 o'clock the next morning in Vladivostok, so programmes made in Moscow are relayed to other places at local viewing times.

Most areas of the Soviet Union offer a wide choice of national and local radio and television stations. There is no radio station for rock music. Soviet teenagers like to listen to popular music, and they are especially fond of music from Britain and the United States. There are some good rock bands in the Soviet Union, and discos are becoming more common.

Fact file: home and leisure

Key facts

Population composition: In 1980 people under 15 years of age made up 24.3 per cent of the population; people between 15 and 59 made up 62.7 per cent; and people over 60 made up 13 per cent. Women formed 53.1 per cent of the population in 1984.

Average life expectancy: 67 years in 1984 (by comparison people in the United States have an average life expectancy of 76 years, whereas people in India live on average 56 years). In 1984 Soviet women had an average life expectancy of 74 years, nine years longer than men.

Rate of population increase: 0.9 per cent per year between 1965 and 1983, less than half the world average. A lower rate of 0.7 a year is forecast for the period 1980–2000. This would give the Soviet Union a population of 375,000,000 by the year 2000.

Family life: The marriage rate in 1983 was 10.3 per 1,000 people. The average number of people in a household was three. Because of the low birth rate, married couples without children must pay a "childless tax" of 6 per cent of their earnings.

Homes: The average size of a town house or apartment is 14.1 sq m (152 sq ft). Rents, payable to the state, are low at 12 per cent of a worker's net income.

Work: The total work force in 1984 was 130,000,000, or 63 out of every 100 people over the age of 15. Women made up 51 per cent of the work force. The five-day working week was introduced in 1967, and since 1970 the average working week has been 39.4 hours. The average working day is 6.93 hours.

Religions: The government discourages religion, and non–religious persons and atheists make up 51.2 per cent of the population. Christians total 25.5 per cent (Russian Orthodox 22.5 per cent, Protestants 1.6 per·cent, Roman Catholics 1.4 per cent); Muslims 11.3 per cent; Jews 1.2 per cent; others 10.8 per cent.

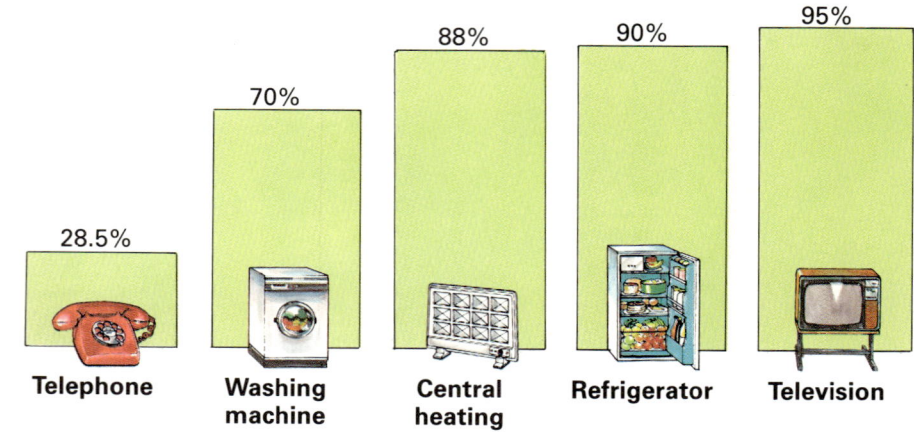

Telephone 28.5%
Washing machine 70%
Central heating 88%
Refrigerator 90%
Television 95%

△ **How many households owned goods in 1986**
Ownership of household goods has increased rapidly in recent years, so that most homes now have televisions (mainly black-and-white), refrigerators and central heating, although fewer than a third have telephones.

Housing and taxes 11%
Goods and other services 12%
Education and culture 15%
Clothing 15%
Alcohol 17%
Food 30%

◁ **How the average household budget was spent in 1986**
Food accounts for nearly a third of household spending in the Soviet Union, with about half as much spent on alcoholic drinks and on clothing.

▽ **Soviet currency**
The unit of currency is the rouble, divided into 100 kopecks. In 1987, there were about 3 roubles to the British pound.

27

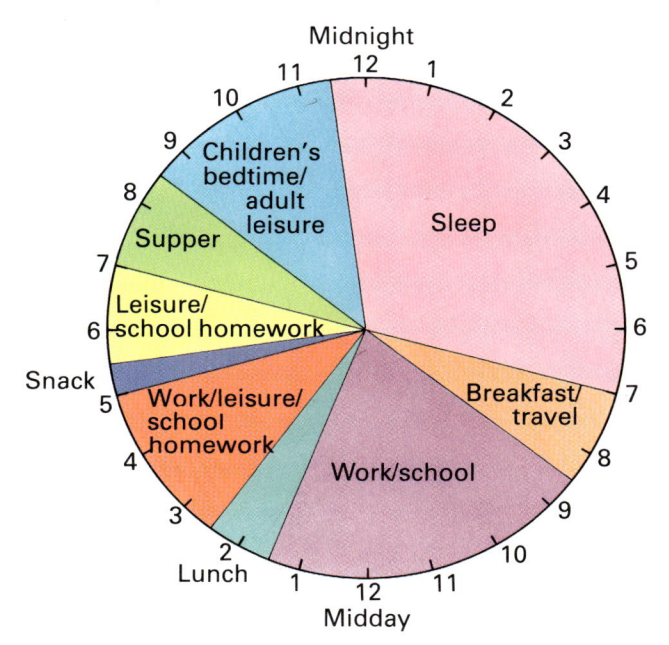

△ How an average family spends a working day

▽ Most popular leisure pursuits
By far the most popular form of entertainment outside the home is the cinema, which had a total audience of nearly 4,000 million people in 1987.

Movies 3,968
Lectures 301
Museums 181
Libraries 146
Concerts 138
Plays 123
(in millions of people)

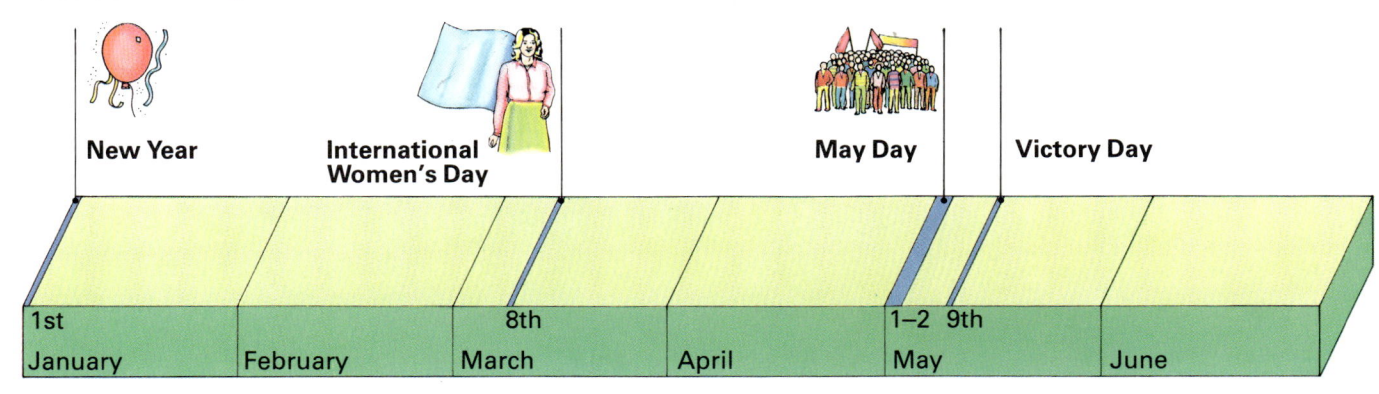

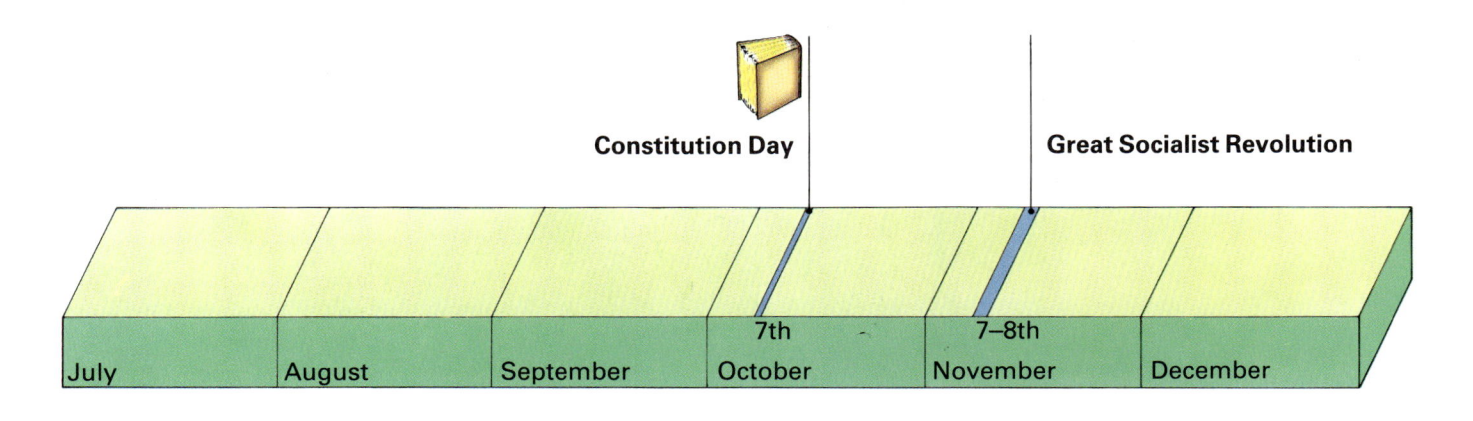

▽ National holidays

- New Year — 1st January
- International Women's Day — 8th March
- May Day — 1–2 May
- Victory Day — 9th June
- Constitution Day — 7th October
- Great Socialist Revolution — 7–8th November

Farming and fishing

After the revolution of 1917 the new Soviet government took over all private land and farms. Two types of farms were established: state farms and collective farms, all of which are owned by the government.

State farms are huge. The average size is about 22,000 hectares (54,400 acres). Most have modern agricultural machinery. The state employs the workers, and provides not only their pay but also housing, schools and clinics.

Collective farms are smaller. They have an average size of 6,000 hectares (14,800 acres). They are jointly owned by all who work on them, and wages are paid as equal shares out of whatever profits the farm makes. Each worker has the right to a plot of land for private use.

Sixty per cent of the Soviet Union's best arable land lies in regions which suffer severe droughts. Crops in the remaining areas are often ruined by storms, and the country often has to import grain. However, the Soviet Union is the world's second largest producer of grain.

Above: A worker with a fine crop of red peppers that have been grown in glasshouses on Yuzhni Collective Farm in the Stavropol Region, near the Caucasus Mountains.

Right: A combine harvester at work in a wheat field, in the southern Ukraine.

The government has a massive land improvement policy. An area of arid land nearly as large as the British Isles has been irrigated and now provides a third of all the Soviet Union's crops. Cotton, rice and grapes grow on land that was once desert or bush.

As recently as the mid-1970s meat was sometimes rationed in parts of the Soviet Union, but production of beef, pork and lamb has risen by 18 per cent since 1982. Estonia, Latvia and Lithuania are the world's leading producers of milk and butter. Pig-breeding is concentrated in the Ukraine, sheep and goats are raised in central Asia and reindeer are herded in Russian Lapland and parts of southern and eastern Siberia.

The Pacific port of Nakhodka is the centre of the Soviet fishing industry. Soviet factory ships buy catches from other countries' small fishing fleets. Soviet fishermen also operate in the Baltic Sea. Sturgeon, which produce the delicacy caviar, are caught in the rivers of the Black and Caspian seas.

Above left: Fish experts examine sterlets, small sturgeon taken from the Amur River in eastern Siberia.

Below: A tea plantation in southern Krasnoyarsk Region.

Above right: Harvesting grapes at Kuban in the southern part of the Krasnoyarsk Region of central Siberia.

Natural resources and industry

Russia before the revolution of 1917 was an underdeveloped country. The Soviet Union now produces one fifth of the world's total industrial output.

The Soviet Union's natural resources are vast. It leads the world in oil production. It has half the world's iron ore, and produces more steel than any other country. It has rich deposits of chromium, cobalt, copper, lead, molybdenum, nickel, platinum, titanium, tungsten and zinc. Mines in Yakutia produce more diamonds than any other country – though mostly of only industrial quality.

Much of Soviet heavy industry is concentrated in the west. There are massive machinery plants near Moscow and Leningrad. Power station equipment is made in Kharkov, Kiev, Riga and Sverdlovsk. Combine harvesters are built in Rostov and automated cotton pickers in Tashkent.

Above: An oil rig in the Caspian Sea off the shore of Azerbaijan Soviet Socialist Republic. This area has been producing oil since the early 1900s, when it was the world's chief oilfield.

Left: Pouring molten steel at one of the Soviet Union's largest steel works at Magnetogorsk. This city is in Chelyabinsk Region, in the southeastern Urals, a great industrial center.

As standards of living have risen in the Soviet Union, so the demand for consumer goods has increased, especially for household electrical appliances. Between 1960 and 1986 annual production of refrigerators rose from fewer than 500,000 to 6,000,000, and that of television sets from 1,000,000 to 10,000,000.

All industry and agriculture in the Soviet Union works to a five-year plan which sets out production targets for each factory and farm for that five-year period. By 1990 the aim is to double the production of clothes and shoes, and improve the supply of spare auto parts to service the large bus and truck industry. The government is also calling for improvements in the quality of finished goods.

In the early 1980s half the Soviet Union's fuel needs were met by home-produced crude oil. But the government now plans to conserve oil supplies and find alternative sources of energy. It is concentrating on the development of natural gas, found in large deposits under the frozen ground inside the Arctic Circle. It is also experimenting with harnessing geothermal, solar and thermonuclear energy.

Above: Open mining of coal at Kholboljinski mine in the Buryat Autonomous Republic, east of Lake Baikal. This region is rich in minerals, such as iron, titanium and tungsten.

Below: Gold, mined in Yakutia, which has two of the country's major goldfields. The Soviet Union is second only to South Africa in the production of this metal.

Soviet Technology

In the years following World War II, Soviet technology concentrated on rebuilding its heavy industries, with the emphasis on power generation and steel making. Then in the 1950s it diverted resources into the aerospace industry. Several hundred spacecraft are launched from the Soviet Union every year. Most of them are artificial satellites intended for communications or meteorological purposes. There are also delivery supply flights carrying crews, food, water and even fresh air to the Soviet Union's orbiting space research stations.

The Soviet Union launched the first artificial Earth satellite, *Sputnik 1*, in October 1957. A month later, *Sputnik 2* carried a dog named Laika beyond the Earth's atmosphere. Two years later *Luna 2* was the first space probe to land on the Moon. Soviet cosmonaut Yuri Gagarin (1934–1968) became the first human being to orbit the Earth in his spacecraft *Vostok 1* in 1961.

Above: The Soviet icebreaker *Lenin* was the world's first non-naval nuclear-powered ship.

Right: A *Soyuz* spacecraft blasts off to carry three Soviet cosmonauts into space. Some *Soyuz* missions have lasted for more than two months and made a thousand orbits of the Earth.

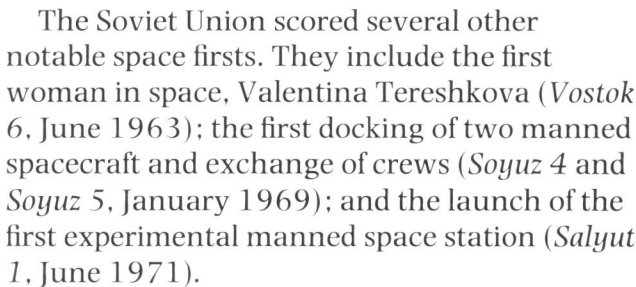

The Soviet Union scored several other notable space firsts. They include the first woman in space, Valentina Tereshkova (*Vostok 6*, June 1963); the first docking of two manned spacecraft and exchange of crews (*Soyuz 4* and *Soyuz 5*, January 1969); and the launch of the first experimental manned space station (*Salyut 1*, June 1971).

New oil and natural gas fields in Kazakhstan, and rich mineral deposits in eastern Siberia, central Asia and the Ukraine have been found, using the information collected on space flights.

Soviet scientists and technologists were also quick to harness nuclear power for peaceful uses. They constructed the first nuclear power station, and the Soviet Union's nuclear-powered icebreakers were the first non-military vessels to use nuclear propulsion. On a large scale, several hydroelectric schemes have been developed to meet industry's increasing requirements for electric power. On a smaller scale, computers are being used for "robots" and automated factories.

Above left: A giant MI-6 helicopter airlifts a portable building across difficult country for workers on the Baikal-Amur Mainline.

Above right: Coloured lights trace out the movements of a cybernetic machine, or "robot".

Below: The Vilnisk power station is one of many hydroelectric projects being developed to meet the needs of Soviet industry.

Transportation

The sheer size of the Soviet Union makes it essential to run an extensive and efficient system of transportation. For example, London is nearer to New York City across the Atlantic Ocean than Moscow is to Vladivostok across Siberia.

The Soviet climate is unkind to roads. In the spring thaw many of them break up because of frost damage and become impassable seas of mud. Distances between major cities are long, and there is still no major west-east highway link. Almost twice as much freight is carried by rail as by truck.

A rail line across Siberia, built between 1891 and 1916, links Moscow and Vladivostok. It runs close to the frontiers with Mongolia and China. In 1984 the Soviets completed a new stretch of line to open up the frozen, mineral-rich region north of Lake Baikal, running to the Amur River and the Pacific coast. It is known as the Baikal-Amur Mainline, or the BAM for short.

Private cars are expensive in the Soviet Union. But public transport, including all internal flights, is good and extremely cheap.

Above: Workers put the finishing touches to a new Vaz 2108 car.

Below left: Building the Baikal-Amur Mainline. The permafrost is so unstable that in places the railbed had to settle for two years before trains could run over it.

Below: A modern high-speed express train waits at Volgograd station. More than half the rail network is electrified.

Above: A station on the Circle Line of the Moscow Metro. This is the most elegant underground system in the world.

Below: A sleigh drawn by reindeer races over the snow near Murmansk, the country's chief Arctic Ocean port.

In parts of the Soviet Union where the climate is less harsh waterways are used for carrying goods. The Volga, which flows into the Caspian Sea, is the main transportation river of Russia. Canals link the Volga to the Baltic Sea, to the River Don and the Black Sea, and to the River Moskva and Moscow. Ice-breaking ships work to keep northern rivers and seaports open in winter, but the most northerly ports become ice-bound and have to be closed from November to March.

Aeroflot, the national airline, has about 7,500 aircraft. This is the biggest fleet of aircraft – all Soviet-built – of any airline in the world. It carries more than 100 million passengers a year to 96 countries, and 4,000,000 tonnes of freight are shipped by air within the Soviet Union. Moscow has four international airports, and there are others at Kiev and Leningrad.

Fact file: economy and trade

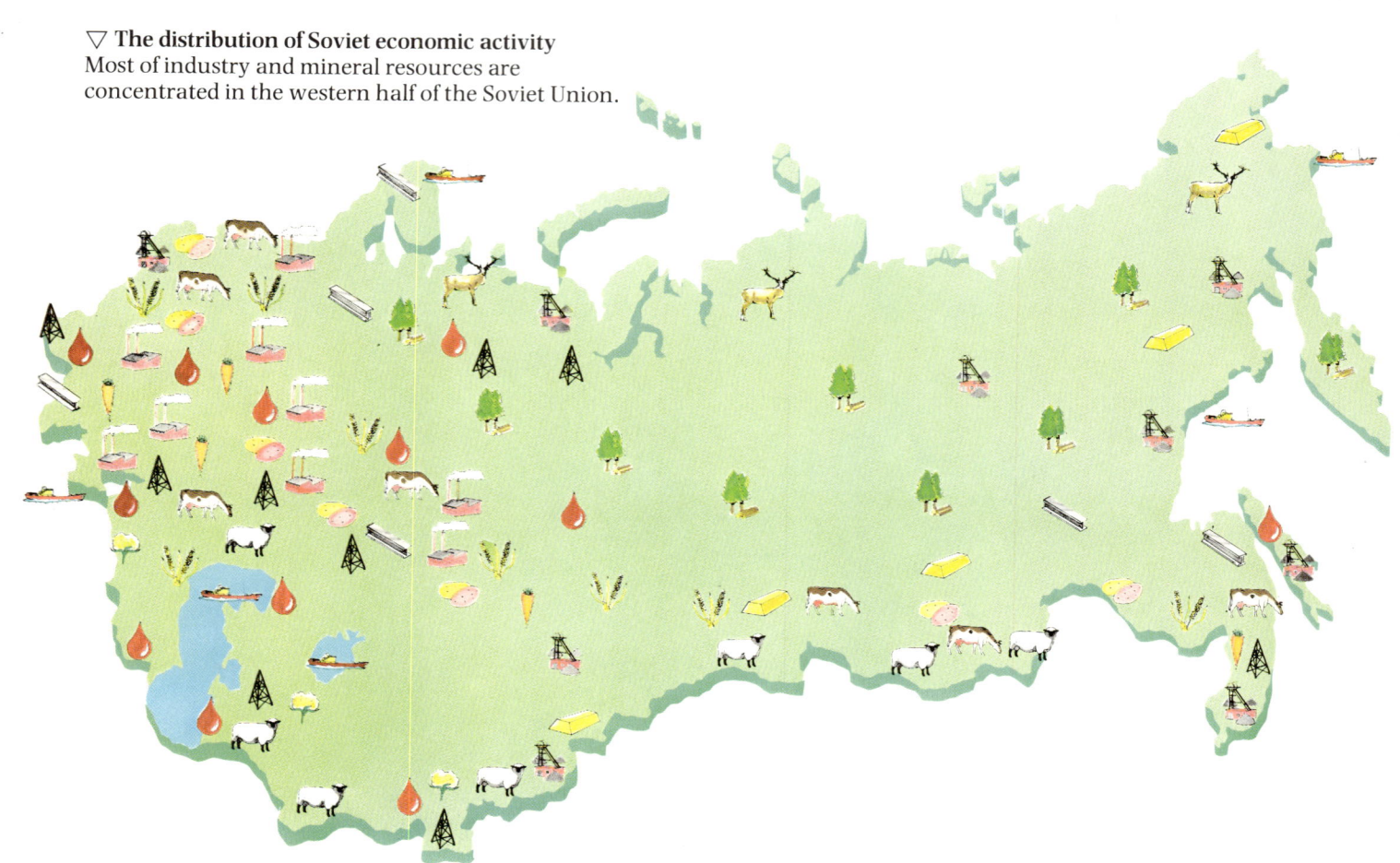

▽ **The distribution of Soviet economic activity**
Most of industry and mineral resources are concentrated in the western half of the Soviet Union.

	Industry
	Petroleum
	Natural gas
	Iron ore
	Coal

	Gold
	Cereals
	Potatoes
	Sugar beet
	Cotton

	Cattle
	Sheep
	Reindeer
	Forest products
	Fishing

Key facts

Structure of production: Of the total net material product (NMP; the total value of goods and the services used in the production of those goods), farming, forestry and fishing contribute 15 per cent, industry 61 per cent and services 24 per cent.
Farming: Land which is continuously cultivated covers 10.5 per cent of the Soviet Union, and grazing land another 16.7 per cent. *Main products*: apples, barley, cotton, dairy products, eggs, maize, meat, potatoes and other vegetables, rye, sugar beet, sunflower seeds, tea, wheat, wool. *Livestock*: cattle 120,900,000; sheep 148,900,000; pigs 77,800,000; horses 5,600,000.
Mining: The Soviet Union is rich in resources. It is the world's leading producer of petroleum and natural gas. It is a major producer of asbestos, bauxite, chrome ore, coal, copper, diamonds, gold, iron ore, lead, manganese, mercury, nickel, silver, tin, tungsten and zinc.
Transportation: *Paved roads*: 793,000 km (493,000 miles); *rail*: 148,000 km (92,000 miles). of which one-third are electrified; *shipping*: 7,095 vessels of 100 gross tonnes or more in 1984; *air*: Aeroflot, the national airline, operates domestic routes and services to more than 90 countries.
Trade (1984): *Total imports*: US $80,352 million; *exports*: $91,492 million.

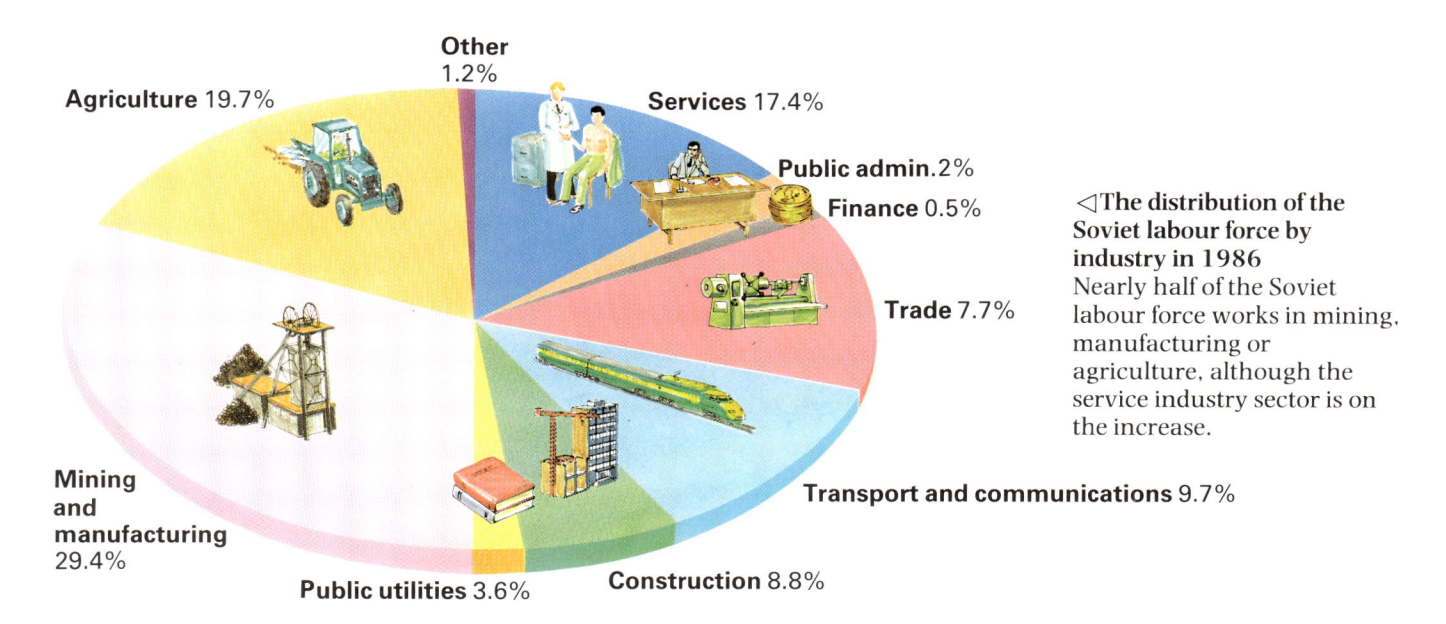

Agriculture 19.7%
Other 1.2%
Services 17.4%
Public admin. 2%
Finance 0.5%
Trade 7.7%

◁ **The distribution of the Soviet labour force by industry in 1986**
Nearly half of the Soviet labour force works in mining, manufacturing or agriculture, although the service industry sector is on the increase.

Mining and manufacturing 29.4%
Public utilities 3.6%
Construction 8.8%
Transport and communications 9.7%

▷ **Soviet Union's main trading partners in 1986** (in percentage of imports/exports)
Other Communist countries in the Eastern bloc accounted for more than 40 per cent of Soviet trade in 1986. Green = imports; brown = exports.

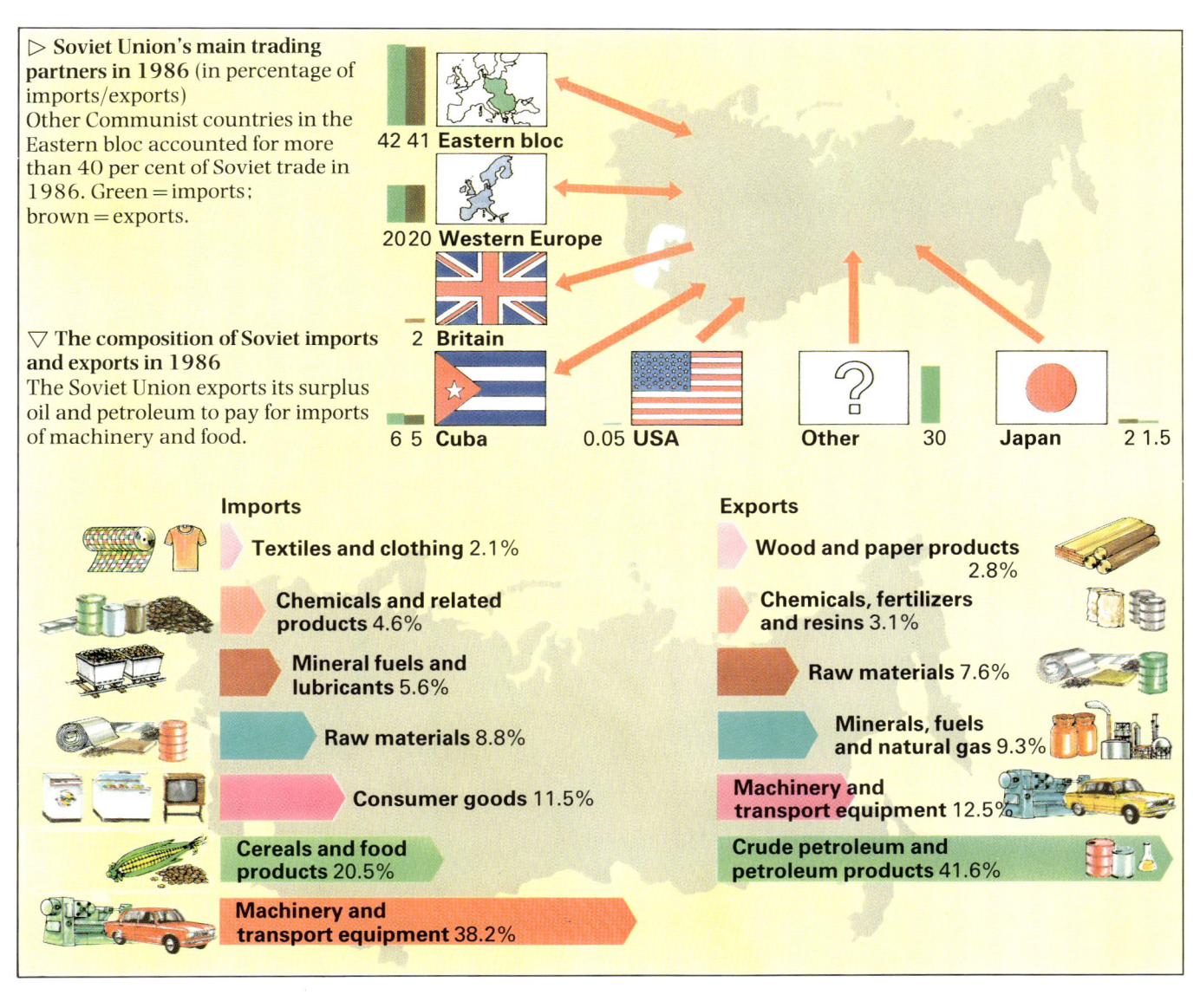

42 41 Eastern bloc
20 20 Western Europe
2 Britain

▽ **The composition of Soviet imports and exports in 1986**
The Soviet Union exports its surplus oil and petroleum to pay for imports of machinery and food.

6 5 Cuba
0.05 USA
Other 30
Japan 2 1.5

Imports
Textiles and clothing 2.1%
Chemicals and related products 4.6%
Mineral fuels and lubricants 5.6%
Raw materials 8.8%
Consumer goods 11.5%
Cereals and food products 20.5%
Machinery and transport equipment 38.2%

Exports
Wood and paper products 2.8%
Chemicals, fertilizers and resins 3.1%
Raw materials 7.6%
Minerals, fuels and natural gas 9.3%
Machinery and transport equipment 12.5%
Crude petroleum and petroleum products 41.6%

Education

All Soviet children receive free, compulsory education between the ages of 6 and 16. Most attend pre-school kindergarten, and continue in further education after they are 16. Even in remote areas, there is a full education service.

Most children attend school six days a week. The school day begins at 8.30 a.m. and ends at 2.30 p.m. Pupils study basic subjects including Russian, mathematics, geography, history, social studies and a foreign language. Hard work, competition and conformity to accepted standards of behaviour are regarded as more important than individual development. Each pupil has a day-book in which teachers write comments and give grades for behaviour and attitude, as well as class work and homework.

Russian is a compulsory subject for every pupil. However, every ethnic minority has the right to teaching and textbooks in its own language. English is the most popular foreign language, followed by German and French.

Above: A State farm kindergarten class in Kazakhstan.

Below: Members of the Young Pioneers gather round a campfire at Bratsk, in Irkutsk.

Right: A Moscow secondary school student uses a computer during a mathematics lesson.

There are three types of secondary schools. Most pupils attend general secondary schools, where they add computer studies and more science subjects to their timetables. Particularly gifted pupils are selected for special secondary schools, where they receive extra tuition in such topics as art, music, languages or electronics. Vocational secondary schools concentrate on subjects, such a mathematics, chemistry or physics, needed for a particular job.

In the two final secondary school years pupils may take a job, and complete their studies by attending a college part time. Their education also continues at work in the form of on-the-job training.

The Soviet Union has more than 4,000 technical colleges and nearly 900 other places of higher education, including 65 universities. At 18 every male must undertake two years' military service. Students may interrupt their studies, but commonly postpone service until after they have graduated. University education is free, but there are 15 applicants for every available place.

Above: Students attending a lecture at the M. V. Lomonosov State University in Moscow. The university was founded in 1755, and today has about 20,000 full-time students.

Below: The exterior of the M. V. Lomonosov University in Moscow. It is generally regarded as the most prestigious of the Soviet Union's 65 universities.

The arts

Outside the Soviet Union, the art of European Russia is best known, but the country has many cultures. The Central Asian republics were part of the great Islamic empires of the 13th century. There is a strong Turkish flavour to Armenian folksongs and dances. Stories and legends from the Baltic republics resemble Scandinavian sagas. In Lapland the Lapps practice traditional handicrafts in bone and leather. In eastern Siberia there are strong Mongol, Chinese and even Japanese influences in art, literature and music.

The most famous Russian paintings are icons, religious pictures painted on wooden panels by artists of the Orthodox Church. In the early years of the 20th century Russian artists experimented with modern styles, but the Soviet government encouraged a straightforward form of painting, which is called "Socialist realism."

Above: An ultra-modern concert hall at Tallinn, the capital of Estonia. The Soviet Union is world famous for the high quality of its musical performances.

Left: A dancer with Moscow's Bolshoi Theatre Ballet makes a spectacular leap. The world of ballet was dominated by Russia during the late 1800s and early 1900s.

Russian music is particularly noted for the operas of such composers as Modest Mussorgsky (1839–1881) and Nikolai Rimsky-Korsakov (1844–1908), and the ballet music of Peter Ilich Tchaikovsky (1840–93) and Igor Stravinsky (1882–1971). Stravinsky, who like many other musicians left the Soviet Union, was one of the most influential 20th century composers. Sergei Prokofiev (1891–1953) and Dmitri Shostakovich (1906–75) remained there.

Anton Chekhov (1860–1904) is regarded as the greatest Russian dramatist. His plays have been translated into every major language. Fyodor Dostoyevsky (1821–81) and Leo Tolstoy (1828–1910) were major novelists. Modern Soviet writers include Boris Pasternak (1890–1960), Mikhail Sholokov (1905–84) and Alexander Solzhenitsyn (1918–   ).

In the 1920s the Soviet government funded films to educate people in the values of Communism. The leading film director of that time was Sergei Eisenstein (1898–1948), whose *Potemkin* (1925) is a cinematic classic.

Above left: A striking mosaic on the wall of a government building at Tashkent, in Uzbekistan.

Above right: A scene from "Ivan the Terrible", a film made in the 1940s by Sergei Eisenstein.

Below: Yevgeny Yevtushenko is a poet whose works comment on today's Soviet society.

The making of the Soviet Union

The Romanov family ruled Russia for more than 300 years. When the last Tsar, Nicholas II, was forced to abdicate in 1917, his country had hardly developed from a medieval, feudal state. The tsars ruled as dictators. Most of the people were treated little better than slaves.

In 1914 Russia joined World War I against Germany and Austria. Nicholas took personal command of his armies, leaving the Tsarina Alexandra to rule. She was under the influence of a dissolute priest, Grigori Rasputin. Russia fell into chaos. Its armies lost battles, and food and fuel were scarce. Workers rioted and went on strike.

In March 1917 soldiers in the capital, Petrograd (now called Leningrad), mutinied. The tsar was forced to abdicate, and a temporary government was set up. An exiled Communist, Vladimir Lenin, returned to Russia and seized power in a second revolution in November, helped by a group of Communists known as Bolsheviks. The Bolsheviks made peace with Germany in 1918, and in 1922 they proclaimed the new Union of Soviet Socialist Republics.

Above: The last Tsar Nicholas II, who came to the throne in 1894, with the Tsarina Alexandra.

Below left: A crowd of Bolsheviks demonstrate.

Below: Vladimir Lenin led the Bolsheviks in the Russian Revolution of November 1917.

After the revolutions of 1917 the country was torn by civil war between the Red Army of the Bolsheviks, led by Lenin's second-in-command, Leon Trotsky, and the White Army of the anti-Communists. The Reds won. Lenin died soon after the new Soviet Union was proclaimed. The Communist secretary-general, Joseph Stalin, seized power.

Stalin introduced a brutal programme of industrialization. *Kulaks*, wealthy peasant farmers, had their lands confiscated, and all farming was organized into collectives. Stalin's secret police removed all his political enemies. It is estimated that 20,000,000 people were murdered, tortured or imprisoned without trial.

In 1941, during World War II, the Germans invaded the Soviet Union. Stalin lived up to his name (it means "steel") as war leader, and the Soviet armed forces played a major part in defeating Germany in 1945.

Above: Posters were often used to convey political messages. One (left) is a Bolshevik campaign poster; the other (right) remembers the starving.

Below: In 1945, just before the end of World War II, Stalin (right) met with Roosevelt of the United States and Churchill (left) of Britain to agree the post-war structure of eastern Europe.

The Soviet Union in the modern world

After World War II, the Soviet government was determined that the country would never again be invaded. It encouraged and supported Communist governments in seven bordering European nations. Under Soviet leadership an "Iron Curtain" was drawn between eastern and western Europe.

Four years after the war ended the Soviet Union had its own atomic bomb to rival the atomic bombs developed by western nations. The Soviet Union and the United States were now the two world superpowers. A "cold war" developed between the Iron Curtain countries and the West, with each side in an arms race to make more and more missiles and other weapons. Stalin died in 1953, and his successors stopped the purges.

Relations with the West then began to improve, as the Soviet Union took an early lead over the United States in the development of rockets and spacecraft. Soviet athletes began to compete in, and sometimes dominate, world sports, and groups of Soviet musicians and dancers toured Europe and North America.

Above: The face of Soviet cosmonaut Yuri Gagarin, in 1961 the first man to travel in space, dominates the Moscow Cosmos Space Pavilion.

Below: The May Day Parade in Moscow's Red Square honours Soviet workers. May 1st and May 2nd are celebrated as national holidays.

During the last twenty years, relations with the West have continued to improve, despite occasional setbacks. In 1968 Soviet troops helped to put down an anti-Communist revolt in Czechoslovakia, and in 1979 they intervened in Afghanistan. In 1985 Mikhail Gorbachev came to power as Soviet leader, and he soon began to introduce a new openness, or *glasnost*, into government, which was designed to modernize the country. People of liberal views, termed dissidents, were released from internal exile.

There are still some shortages – of homes and cars, for example – and economic problems remain. Some internal dissent continues, but minority groups have been allowed to hold demonstrations to express openly their grievances. In the late 1980s, disarmament talks between the Soviet and American governments brought new hope for world peace.

Left: A Soviet tank, manned by Afghan soldiers, guards Kabul airport in January 1980.

Above: In October 1986 Soviet leader Gorbachev and American President Reagan met in Iceland for disarmament talks.

Below: A thousand Crimean Tartars were allowed to demonstrate in Moscow in July 1987.

Fact file: government and world role

The Union of Soviet Socialist Republics (USSR) is a federation of 15 separate republics.

Key facts

Official name: *Soyuz Sovyetskikh Sotsialistcheskikh Respublik* (Union of Soviet Socialist Republics).
Flag: Red, with a gold hammer and sickle in the upper corner near the staff. Above the hammer and sickle is a gold-bordered, five-pointed star.
National anthem: *Soyuz nerushimy respublik svobodnykh* ("The Unbreakable Union of Free Republics").
National government: Power is shared between the Communist Party, which makes policies, and the national government, which carries them out.
Communist Party: About 5,000 delegates from party groups form the All-Union Party Congress, which meets every five years. It elects a Central Committee, which meets every six months, which in turn chooses the Politburo (Political Bureau) and the Secretariat, which carry on day-to-day work. The General Secretary of the Central Committee heads the Politburo and the Secretariat, and is the most powerful person in the country.
Legislature: the Supreme Soviet, which meets twice a year and consists of two chambers, the Council of the Union and the Council of Nationalities, each with 750 members elected for five-year terms. The Supreme Soviet elects from among its members the Presidium, a 39-strong body which handles legislation when the Supreme Soviet is not in session. Its chairman serves as head of state. The Supreme Soviet also chooses the Council of Ministers, whose chairman serves as prime minister.
Local government: Each of the 15 Union Republics has its own supreme soviet, presidium and council of ministers. Four Union Republics include similarly governed Autonomous Republics: there are 16 in the RSFSR, two in Georgia, one in Azerbaijan and one in Uzbekistan.
Armed forces: At least two years' military service is compulsory for males. In 1985 the total strength of the armed forces was more than 5,000,000, with around 25,000,000 in the reserves and 500,000 in security and border forces. In 1983 about 29 per cent of the Soviet Union's gross national product went on military expenditure.
Economic alliance: The Soviet Union is the leading member of the Council for Mutual Economic Assistance (COMECON), to which nine other countries belong.

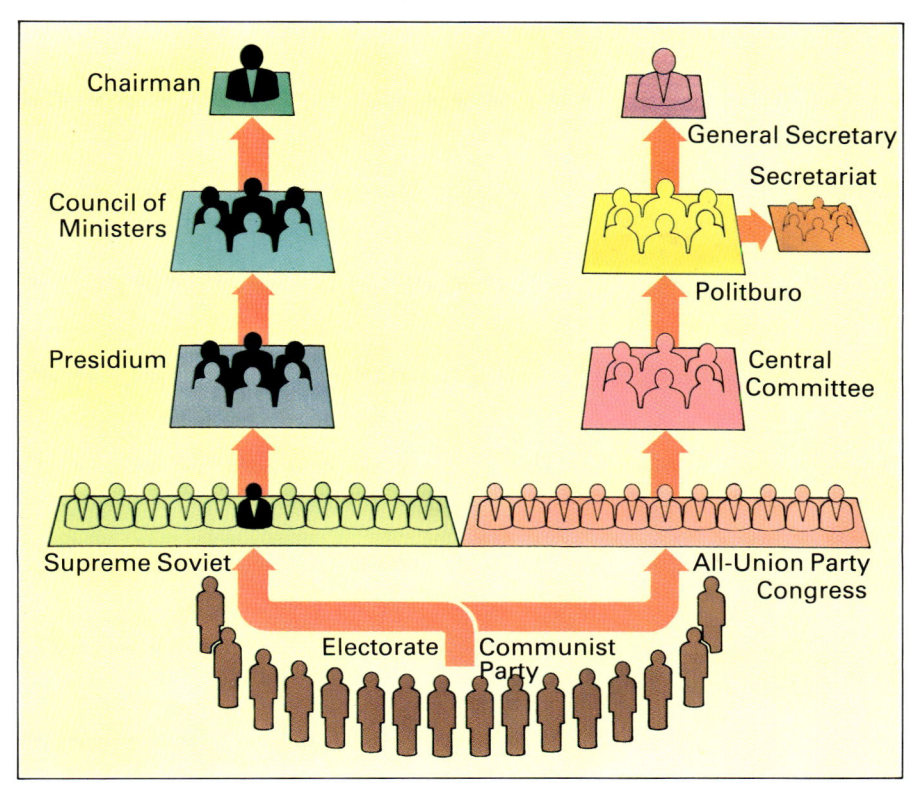

◁ **The Soviet government**
The head of state is the Chairman of the Presidium, and the Prime Minister is the Chairman of the Council of Ministers. Neither is as powerful as the General Secretary of the Secretariat and Politburo.

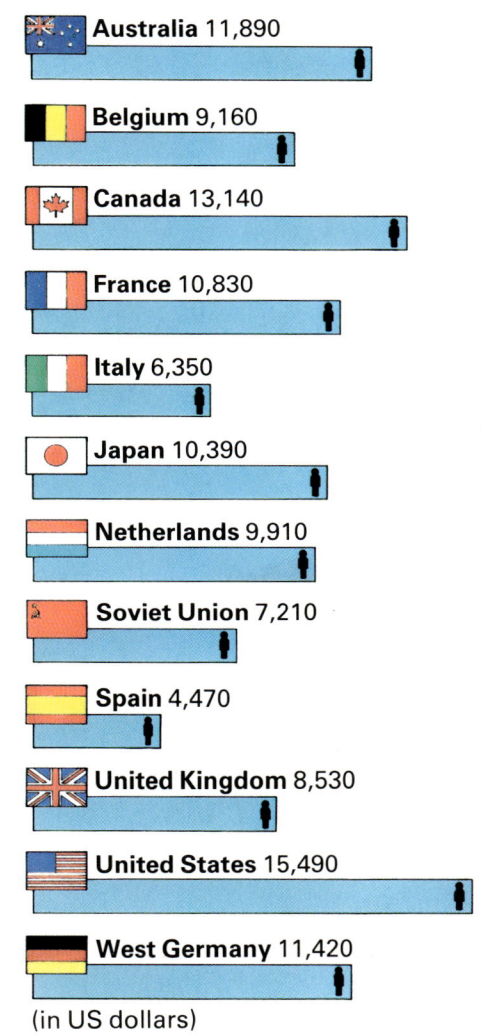

▽ **The Eastern bloc**
Six European countries on the USSR's western border – known as the Eastern bloc – have Communist governments which largely follow Soviet policies. Together with the USSR, they form the nations of the Warsaw Pact.

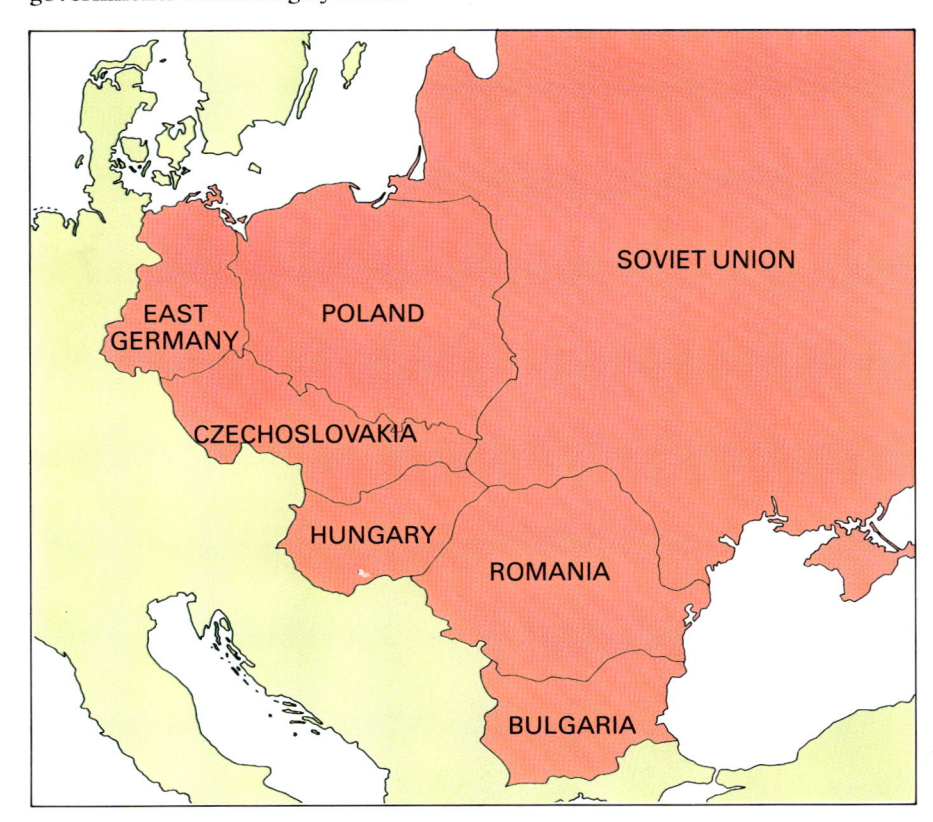

Australia 11,890
Belgium 9,160
Canada 13,140
France 10,830
Italy 6,350
Japan 10,390
Netherlands 9,910
Soviet Union 7,210
Spain 4,470
United Kingdom 8,530
United States 15,490
West Germany 11,420

(in US dollars)

△ **National wealth created per person in 1986**
Despite the USSR's tremendous national resources and industrial capacity, its standard of living is less than that of Britain and less than half of that of the United States.

Index

agriculture 10
alcoholism 20, 21
Alma-Ata 14
alphabets, 8, 9
Altai Mountains 7
Amur River 23, 29, 34
Angara River 7
apartments 11, 16
Armenia 8, 9, 14, 40
Ashkhabad 14
Azerbaijan 11, 14, 30

Baikal-Amur Mainline 33, 34
Baikal, Lake 5, 7, 11, 34
Baku 11, 14
Baltic Sea 29, 35
birth rate 16
Black Sea 8, 23, 29, 35
bliny 21
Bolsheviks 42–43
bomb, atomic 44
borscht 21

cars 34,
Caspian Sea 7, 14, 29, 30, 35
chess 22, 23
"childless tax" 16, 26
climate 14, 34
coal 31, 36
"cold war" 44
COMECON 46
Communist Party 12, 17, 24, 46
computers 33, 38
Council of Ministers 46
crops 28–29

dacha 13
dastarhan 17
diamonds 30, 36
Dnepropetrovsk 14
Don River 35
Dostoyevsky, Fyodor 41
Dushanbe 14
Dzhugdzhur Mountains 7

earnings 17
energy 31, 36
Estonia 9, 10, 14, 29
exports 36, 37

farms 28, 36, 43
films 22, 41
fishing 29
five-year plan 31
Frunze 10, 14

Gagarin, Yuri 32, 44
gas, natural 31, 33
Georgia 8, 14
glasnost 45
gold 31, 36
Gorbachev, Mikhail 45,
Gorky 14

homes 11, 16, 26
household equipment 16, 31
hydroelectric scheme 33,

icebreaker 32, 33, 35
imports 36, 37
income tax 17
"Iron Curtain" 44
irrigation 29
Izvestia 24

Kazakhstan 14, 21, 38
Kharkov 14, 30
Khirgizia 10, 14
Kiev 8, 14, 30, 35
kindergarten 38
Kishinev 14
Kremlin 12–13
Krokodil 24
Kuibyshev 14

land area 14
languages 8, 14, 22, 38
Lapland, Soviet 29, 40
Latvia 9, 14, 29
Lena River 14
Lenin, Vladimir I, 5, 13, 42, 43
Leningrad 5, 14, 30, 35
life expectancy 26
literacy 24
literature 40
Lithuania 9, 14, 29

machinery 30
manufacturing 36
marriage 11, 16, 26
mechanization 10
Metro, Moscow 13, 35
military service 39, 46
minerals 30, 33, 36
mining 30, 36
Minsk 6, 14
Moldavia 14
Moscow 5, 8, 11, 12–13, 14, 16, 20, 23, 24, 25, 30, 34, 35, 39, 44
Moskva River 12, 35
music 25, 40–41
Mussorgsky, Modeste 41

naan bread 21
newspapers 24
Nicholas II 42,
Novosibirsk 14
nuclear power 30, 33

oil 31, 30, 33

Pacific Ocean 6
painting 40
Palace of Congresses 12
palov 21
Pamir Mountains 7, 14
Pasternak, Boris 41

permafrost 6
physical training 23
piroshki 21
Politbureau 46
population 10, 14, 15, 26
power stations 30
Pravda 24
prices 26
production 36
Prokoviev, Sergei 41

radio 24, 25
railroads 34, 36
Rasputin, Grigory 42
rationing 29
Red Square 13, 44
religions 9, 26
residence permits 11
revolution 5, 13, 30, 42–43
Riga 14, 30
Rimsky-Korsakov, Nikolai 41
rivers 7
roads 36
Romanov family 42
Rostov 30
RSFSR 14

Samarkand 9, 16
samovar 20, 21
shchi 20
shipping 36
Sholokov, Mikhail 41
Shostakovich, Dmitri 41
Siberia 6, 7, 10, 17, 29, 40
soccer 22, 23
Solzhenitsyn, Alexander 41
spacecraft 32–33, 44
sport 27
Stalin, Joseph 43, 44
stamp collecting 22
standard of living 31
Stanovoi Mountains 7
steel 30
Stravinsky, Igor 41
supermarket 19
Supreme Soviet 12, 46
Sverdlovsk 14, 30

Tadzhikistan 14, 23
taiga 6
Tallinn 9, 10, 14, 40
Tamerlane 9
Tashkent 14, 18, 30, 41
TASS, news agency 24
Tbilisi 14
Tchaikovsky, Peter Ilich 41
tea 20, 29
television 16, 24, 25
temperature 6, 13
Tereshkova, Valentina 33
time difference 6, 25
Tolstoy, Leo 41
track and field 23
trade unions 23

Trotsky, Leon 43
tundra 6
Turkmenistan 7, 9, 14, 17, 21

Ukraine 8, 14, 28–29
universities 39
Ural Mountains 7
Uzbekistan 9, 14, 16, 18, 21, 41

vacations 23
Verkhoyansk Mountains 7
Vilnius 14
Vladivostok 6, 25, 34
vodka 21
Volga River 14, 35

wages 19
Warsaw Pact 46
waterways 35
world wars 42, 43

Yakutia 6, 23, 30, 31
Yerevan 14
yurt 17